Knickers, oop t'nick, Pussydream, Popham Down,
Mollyblobs, Point the Horse, Mumpers Hide; what do
you call *your* house? House namers have used an
astonishing range of names from Ackybotha to Zeelust
in their search to express individuality. More thought is
often given to the choice of house name than to any
other type of name and few other names are so
uninhibited, inventive or at times so disastrous. This
book unlocks many of the secrets of house names. It is
an entertaining, often humorous, book which is also a
comprehensive reference to the subject.

Joyce Miles has researched the subject of house
names for several years. She has written one other
book on the subject. Her main interest is travelling as
often and as far as possible – collecting house names
in the process.

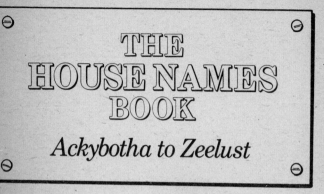

THE HOUSE NAMES BOOK

BOOK

Ackybotha to Zeelust

JOYCE MILES

London
UNWIN PAPERBACKS
Boston   Sydney

First published in Unwin Paperbacks 1982

UNWIN® PAPERBACKS
40 Museum Street, London, WC1A 1LU, UK

Unwin Paperbacks
Park Lane, Hemel Hempstead, Herts HP2 4TE, UK

George Allen & Unwin Australia Pty Ltd.,
8 Napier Street, North Sydney, NSW 2060, Australia

British Library Cataloguing in Publication Data

Miles, Joyce C.
    The House Names Book.
1. Dwellings – Names
I. Title
643".1   GT471
ISBN 0-04-827046-6

Set in 10 on 11 point Souvenir by Performance Typesetting Ltd
and printed in Great Britain
by Richard Clay (The Chaucer Press) Ltd, Bungay Suffolk

ACKNOWLEDGEMENTS

I would like to thank the Cultural Department of the Belgian Embassy, London, and Mr Oliver Padel of the Institute of Cornish Studies for help with translations. I am also extremely grateful to all the people who have not only given me many cups of tea and much encouragement, but have provided the hundreds of amusing, astonishing and spectacular house names that have made this book possible.

CONTENTS

From Burghers to Wimpey

A story behind every name

KNICKERS, oop t'nick, Pussydream, Popham Down, Mollyblobs, Barley Picle, Point the Horse, Mumpers Hide; what do you call *your* house? Perhaps it doesn't yet have a name and you are simply looking for one. If so you are about to join the self-revealing and endlessly ingenious world of house namers.

Our lives are dominated by national insurance numbers, telephone numbers, car registrations and cashpoint numbers. The Post Office usually likes you to have a house number, except in rural areas where this is not possible. But there is no reason generally why your house, whether you own it or rent it from a private landlord or the council, should be without a name. Noble lords, notorious villains, solid citizens, fearful snobs and ordinary folk have named huts, hovels, mansions, villas and unassuming homes from early times.

It seems a little half-hearted to name all the dogs and children, but to leave unnamed the place where they all live. A house name expresses individuality and brightens the lives of passers-by. Sometimes it can do more, revealing a flash of imagination or bringing out an echo of history. People often give more thought to the choice of house names than to any other type of name, and no other names are so eloquent of everything from a lifetime's hopes to snobbery or defiance of relatives and neighbours. Few other names are so uninhibited, inventive or at times so disastrous, and very many have more of a story behind them than appears at first sight.

Whether you are racking your brains to choose a name for your own home or baffled by some strange inscription on your neighbour's front door, you should find this book enlightening, and I hope useful. After several years of research into many thousands of house names and their origins I am beginning to realise how inexhaustibly varied they are, and how fascinating are some of the thoughts and speculations they can stimulate.

Unlikely as it may sometimes seem, all the names quoted as examples in this book do exist and have been verified by me in the course of my research. They are reproduced exactly as they were found. If you are disposed to doubt this, go out and look at a few yourself.

The Clever Ones

A HIGHLY developed sense of humour, a vivid imagination or just sheer inspiration have led to some quite astonishing names. One house name itself might sum up this category – Whod'athoutit?

Woodworm's Hilton was named on account of the luxurious living the pests were having on the beams when new owners moved in. Binkasenvi arose when a person nicknamed Binka remarked how envious she was of her friend's new home. Perkin Warbeck (the Pretender) was chosen as the owners said that at the time they had the house built they pretended they could afford it.

Some names display a sophisticated degree of verbal wit – Isomer, for example, means 'sharing equally', Inter Nos – between us, and the musical term Portamento, 'a gliding or passing from one pitch to another' reflected the owners' nomadic lives.

The advertisement for their bargain home in the *Birmingham Evening Mail* led one young couple to name their home Admail after the column that carried the advertisement.

Broadgate Cottage has two front entrances, and after innumerable enquiries the owners have been driven to labelling the second entrance Broadgate Cottage Too. At The Nutshell they have a cat called Colonel, and No. 10 is called Downing.

Occasionally the name of a house will be linked with the name of the road it is situated in: hence Pan Yan on Picklers Hill, The Pilgrims in Chaucer Road, Tadpole House in Frog Grove Lane, Dry Spot in Wet Lane and Offshoot in Knightchute Lane. In Coffeelake Meadow there is a Maxwell House and a Samovar in Creampot Lane. Dickens Roads often have a Bleak House or a Copperfield. Timberline (named after a motel in Canada on the timber line), links with its location betwen Timber Hill and Timber Vale; and here also is Lumberlayers. One of the most apt is Pepran, Saltbox Road and what about El-Sanne in Bogs Lane?

Some names connect directly with villages – for example Little Scratch is in Itchington, Topple is at Over, the village of Pityme in Cornwall has Pity-me-Not and The Wee Wee House is at Wyre Piddle.

It is better not to enquire too deeply into Myob (and certainly not Myobb) otherwise there is a danger of being told to mind one's own business. Some users of this name may have been influenced by the deeper significance it carries in the brilliantly satirical science fiction story *And Then There Were None* by Eric Frank Russell which first appeared about 1951. Here Myob has a double meaning as the key word of a social code in which you refuse to answer stupid questions and pay your way in life by exchanging obligations with others. A tempting thought for a tempting name.

Kwitchurbelyakin is enough to stop anyone in his tracks.

· Inviting Names ·

SOME people do their utmost to make the stranger welcome – either by using the actual word in names such as The Welcome or Welcome Cottage, or just standing on its own – Welcome, although this occasionally turns up as a back-spelling – Emoclew, as does Tamrood. Whether these set out to puzzle visitors or imply that they should turn back is anybody's guess.

In recent years the concept of 'welcome' has appeared in a variety of languages as a house name – Benvenuto, Bon Accueil and Willkommen. The Welsh welcome – Croeso – can be found more or less all over the UK.

Chai Char (a cup of tea) is in a lane called Journey's End. At Wassailing they wanted an attractive name and ended up with this rather jolly one. In Old English it was a form of salutation – 'be in good health', but its modern definition suggests a festive occasion or a drinking bout. Yam Seng is thought to be a Chinese form of 'bottoms up'. Chinwags and Gossips positively invite people to drop in. Bacchanalia suggests a really good time being had by all and Hicbibby is intended to mean 'Here I drink'.

There are manufactured forms of invitation, often found at the seaside, but not exclusively so – Kumincyde, Poppin, Takitezy, Dukumin, Avarest, Stepaside, Tarryawhile, Byd-a-Wee (sometimes found beautifully lettered in gold leaf on a fanlight.) In-Vi-Ted is a clever use of family names. We-r-In and Yer-We-Be suggest you would not call at the house in vain.

Cosy Nook and Cosy Cot (with several variations in spelling such as Kosikot and Kosineuk) used to be very popular, but are less so today. Instead the preference seems to be for words like Osokosie or The Snuggery.

Out of the Way

WHAT leads people to choose seemingly extraordinary names? Pussydream at first seems almost unbelievable. There is, however, usually a perfectly good explanation for most names. Pussydream came about because the owners first chose a name that the Post Office thought would cause confusion as there was already a house so named in that area. Somewhat disappointed, the family then set to work to seek out a name that would be so outrageous that it would once again be rejected. Pussydream was the answer. Unfortunately for them it was accepted and they are now stuck with it!

Shaggs Flood is built next to land known as Shaggs Lawn, and there is a stream now running in a culvert which might well have flooded in years past.

Bell Rope stands on land which was given to the local church and the rent obtained from it went towards the upkeep of the church bells. Wideawake is at the top of a hill, with windows that suggest wide open eyes.

A great deal went wrong during the construction of The Bungle, and in spite of careful instructions the wrong fireplaces were installed at Rongrates.

It was intended that Mumpers Hide should have been Beggars Roost, but when the latter name was found on several houses in the locality synonyms for both words were chosen – mumpers being beggars and a hide serving as a roost.

Allboys owners had four sons, and Telemark, a dance step, was chosen by a teacher of dancing. First Site was the first house to be built on that particular development.

Virgins Living has a very long history. In the Middle Ages a family named Virgin owned and made a living from the land on which the house is built, parts of which date from 1450.

Knickers was the result of someone being rather impressed by a house called Cobblers and wanting to go one better. Perhaps it should be added rather hastily that there are many houses quite legitimately called Cobblers as shoemakers once lived there.

An old salt once lived at Fujimar and was anxious to assure everyone that he was all right.

· Architectural ·

THE house owner who wants a name to serve as a ready means of identification will seize gratefully on almost any distinctive feature that can be seen from the road – Long Eave, Strawtop, Singlestack, Quoin, Flat Roof House, Twisted Chimneys, Windows (it has eleven in the front alone), Double Gates, The Bent House, The Clock House, Dormers (one even has a deliberate misspelling – Doormirs). Staddlestones (usually with several old staddlestones in the garden) – there are hundreds of such examples, but by far the most favoured over the years has been 'gables' in a variety of forms. From The Gables which you can still find on many houses of 1910 vintage, the idea has been developed and varied and a house with an imposing roofline today is more likely to be called Four Gables, Wood Gables, Green Gables or South Gable. There is even one called Gable Hid. The House of Seven Gables, built at Salem in Massachusetts in 1668, was put under a curse at the witchcraft trials and was used by the American novelist Nathaniel Hawthorne as the setting for his famous novel *The House of the Seven Gables*, written in 1851.

When land was more readily available than it is today, and the idea of ownership of land had a certain snob appeal, a proud owner would emphasise his status (or hopes of status) with names such as Two Acres, Broad Acres or Longacres, but when, as is usually the case nowadays, an acre is shared by up to a dozen plots, then Acre End is more applicable. The Squeeky Bit is an apt use of a dialect name.

Names derived from fields and meadows – Meadow View, Green Field, Fieldside – have long been favourites, but in many areas such names would be impossible and in recent years there has been a tendency to turn for inspiration to the actual material used in the construction of the property – Bricks (with alternative spellings such as Brix or Briques), Cattybrook named after the actual company supplying the bricks, Old Stocks (stocks being best-quality clamp-burnt bricks), Clinkers (hard bricks used for paving); tiles in various colours – Greentiles, Bluetiles, Greytiles; Pantiles, Granite Villa, Flintstones, Grouan House (a Cornish mining term for rough pebbles) and Chippings after loose chippings in the drive.

Twinstax is skilfully allusive. Although the house has two chimney stacks, the name is derived from the refund of tax and a large sum from the insurance company on the birth of twins, which formed the down payment on the house.

I had expected perhaps to find a drinker at Double Diamond, but this name only refers to two ornamental brickwork diamonds in either gable. Similarly, Black Diamonds has a diamond pattern in black in the brickwork.

If you have a stone lion or other heraldic beast it seems ungrateful to ignore him, though it is more of a problem if your neighbour has his head and front paws while the rear end sticks out of the hole in your hedge. It is only a matter of time before someone turns up with two lions and a Corner House. Lion Cottage has a magnificent stone lion sitting above its porch; Griffon House is guarded by a terracotta griffon; but although Griffins has a number of stone animals in the garden, this word can also mean 'newcomers' which, at the time of naming the house, was appropriate. Wheel Cottage has an old wheel outside and the sign at Golden Key is appropriately illustrated. In the front garden of Stoney Seat is a stone bench of almost megalithic aspect.

The structure of the land on which a house is built is, of course, all important, but few geological names appear. In the early part of the century one house was called Oolite, and there are a number with names such as Chalkpit Piece and Marle Cottage (Redmarley, incidentally, has nothing to do with either colour or soil, but means open land near a reedy lake), but the main interest here lies in sand and stone. Stone, with more possibilities for puns and money jokes, and more associations of permanence, is the more popular and besides those who chose Stone House, Stonewalls or Greystones, there are those who apparently have to suffer Stoneyacres, Stoneyfield or just Stones. Others have found it appropriate to call their houses Sandy Piece, Sandyhills, Sandfield, Sandy Brook – one hopeful gardener has gone as far as calling his house Sahara to indicate the state of the land when he attempted to lay out a garden. On the other hand, one owner was so delighted with his plot that he dubbed it Joyous Earth which perhaps has a slightly Arthurian ring, and perhaps just gets away with it.

Apart from the more obvious features of a house which might serve as the base for a name – Tall Chimneys, Timber Top or Two Gates, for example, there are sometimes other aspects of the property that owners feel worth mentioning. Dwand is dry, warm and no draughts; the owner of Lautrec is not a lover of art – just proud of the fact that he has two loos – one up and one down. Not only was Walkabout built by an Australian (where aborigines are said to go off into the bush for weeks at a time on 'walkabouts') but the house is so planned that it is possible to walk about the spacious ground floor with comfort. Slice Cottage was Orchard View, until the orchard was built on. Its present name emphasises its semi-detached ground plan.

Sometimes there are certain disadvantages of a house that so infuriate the owner that he labels the house almost in disgust. Igloo is extremely cold (although when I found this name also in Portugal the temperature was over 30°C so someone there had a sense of humour). Some owners like to emphasise a house's peculiarities – Kraziesteps and Dizzy Heights are perched up on steep cliffs; Curiosity Cottage has a variety of styles of windows and building materials; Nothing Matches refers to its internal finishings and Bendor-bump had very low beams.

Curiously enough, The Shambles and Chaos (or its variants such as Equal Chaos and Kaos) usually have beautiful signs attached to immaculate houses. Bedlam refers to its inhabitants – as once did Hellzapoppin when all the children were young.

The Shack, Our Shed, Ol's Ole are sometimes, but not always, the reverse of the pompous Victorian habit of seeking to dignify a poky residence with a mighty name. The present day Shack may very well have a Rolls in the drive.

Pride of Ownership

PRIDE of ownership is natural, more especially in one's first home which is, after all, perhaps the most expensive and one of the most important events so far experienced. If the search has been a long one then the cry of triumph will result in Eureka, At Last (in one case this was after a particularly difficult battle for a building permit), Atlasta (invented when a suitable plot of land was found after much searching), Enfin, Found, Treksend, Trails End, Dunlukin and Hunters End. Those who have actually wielded a pick and shovel or mixed cement and carried hods of bricks around sometimes wish to record this in names such as Mayditte, The Tyro, Wedydit or, in the case of a house built by a father and his two sons, Ladsani. Ard-Cum-Bi, Hardearned and Ardwun reflect the hard struggle the owners had before becoming property owners. One of the most original here is Tuksumduin.

Other people choose to display their joy in owning a house in names like R'Place, Tizours, My Owne, ImzNerz, Owzitis, Hisn'ers, Ersanmyne, Ourouse, Ourome, Ourownia and Ourown.

Olcote is 'our little corner of the earth'. A vicar and his family, having spent all their lives in church vicarages, named their first private home The Roof Tree as they now had not only a shelter but also one with a large beam in the roof.

Personal
Names

YOU can have a lot of fun inventing a house name
from either family forenames or surnames. However, a word
of warning – check that you do not do as Irene and Albert
did and end up with Renal. Phyllis and Bertram changed
their minds.

Some are obvious at first glance – Janbaz, Iverne,
Chapeg, Gladjon, Dy-Anjo and Samphylan, but some need
translation. Shapaudra comes from Sharon, Pat, Paul and
Sandra; Rusper (also the name of a Sussex village so here
the owners had two personal associations) is from Richard,
Stephen, Paul and Rachael; Joberatre is from John, Bet,
Ray and Trev; Marverene is from Margaret, Vernon and
Irene and The Ellpad belongs to Ellen and Paddy which is
clever as the word 'pad' is now associated with a place to

live. Blended names are a fairly recent fashion. When house naming first became popular the single forename was often used – Algernon Villa, Georgina House, Eustace Lodge – the names themselves following the then current fashion in personal names. These were later superseded by Gertiville, Claudeville and Normanhurst. Today you are more likely to see Kateholm, Wendycot or Davisal.

Surnames can be similarly adapted – Miss Williams marrying Mr Markham has a choice of Wilmar or Markiams; Mr Grice married Miss Lord and they live at Griord. However, when Miss Martin married Mr Giles they chose to use the two initials 'm' and 'g' and ended up with Emange, which pronounced as a complete word, is not quite what they expected. Dorsanos can also easily be mis-pronounced. It is Dor's and O's (Dorothy's and Owen's).

If, of course, you have the type of surname that lends itself, then you can be even more clever – the Redheads live at Coppernob; the Cheese family at The Mousetrap; the Flowers at Flowers Bloom; the Bees at The Hive; the Nutts at The Nut House; the Badgers at The Sett. Mr and Mrs Wall and two daughters live at Four Walls, the Dingleys at Dingley Dell. People named Bird are often inspired – they live at houses with names such as The Nest, Magpies, Wild Wings, Wayfarers and Finches Nest.

The Gammon family have been particularly inventive, having named one house Rashers and another Trotters (and, incredibly, once having a cook called Violet Pig!).

If you choose to invent your housename from the names of your family, then at least you have got something very personal. If you sell your house the future owners may well have to change the name, but you can always take the nameplate with you.

Transferred Names

ONE of the surprises about house names is the huge popularity of the transferred place name (e.g. a house in Rawtenstall called Lyndhurst, or one in Torquay called Royston). Numerically this is the largest source of house names. Perhaps on reflection this is not so surprising, if one remembers how many house names tell part of someone's life story. There is a little bit of the colonising spirit in all of us, and calling one's Cornish bungalow Barnsley is not unlike the behaviour of those explorers who could scarcely wait to drop anchor before distributing familiar names along the unknown coastline before them.

Some owners choose the name of the town in which they were born, and so Rugby ends up in Gloucestershire and Malvern goes out to Australia. In some cases there is a blend of names – at Wellsburn she came from Wells and he came from Burnham-on-Sea; Sheffern is invented from Sheffield and Colerne. In Somerset there is a Manxmaid. Bodstell is situated midway between Bodmin and St. Austell.

Changing fashions in the use of names from holiday resorts provide a revealing marginal comment on the social history of the last two hundred years. By the end of the eighteenth century people were enjoying visits to seaside resorts like Brighton and Scarborough and trips into the country, and these increased with the coming of the railways. Houses bore names like Chester House, Bath Cottage, Thanet Cottage and York House. In 1841 Thomas Cook introduced his first excursion from Leicester to Loughborough, then to Snowdonia and Scotland. From the middle of the nineteenth century transferred place names for houses were being selected from a much wider area than before, reflecting the growth of tourism. Walsall, for example, had a number of houses in the 1870s with Scottish place names. Foreign place names like Sorrento and Cairo began to appear. By the 1930s paid holidays and home ownership were on the increase and many of the houses on estates had names like Tenby, Clevedon, Lyme Regis and Conway on their gateposts (although the very popular places like Blackpool, Rhyl, Southend and Margate inspired very few). The package holiday has opened up the Continent to millions and so today we see many houses bearing names such as Marbella, Tossa, Lloret, Torremolinos and Amalfi.

As the tour operators get more ambitious the names come from further afield – Samarkand, Serengeti and Barbados. A few, of course, come as a result of owners working abroad – Inyanga, Tregannu, Solna, Kowloon, Kenya, Mandalay and Kuwait – in fact from almost all over the world.

What might be termed 'royal' names – Windsor, Balmoral, Sandringham and Coppins – do occur from time to time, although the first three are more often found as street names. The media of mass communication have made remote places familiar to everyone and so much that would have seemed exotic or presumptuous on ordinary homes a century ago is now accepted as the normal level of sophistication.

It is, however, sometimes a little startling to find Llandudno in Cornwall and Polperro in Bradford.

Not only are place names transferred but lakes, rivers, hills, mountains, fjords, dams – almost any named geographical feature is suitable. The Fishawack, for example, is the old Indian name for a river in New Jersey, USA, where the owner of the house so named spent much of her early life. Kanchenjunga, Mont Blanc, Jungfrau, Everest – names of mountains make frequent appearances – perhaps the acquisition of their own homes has, for some, been the equivalent of climbing the highest peaks. Nothing short of the world's highest active volcano – Cotopaxi – would do in one case, although perhaps it was the poem that provided the inspiration. Certainly at Darien they have a good view of the surrounding countryside.

Before the jet age many a large cruise liner gave its name to a house – sometimes a reminder of a honeymoon – Chusan, Oronsay, Devonia; occasionally a hotel will be remembered – Pinimar, Cawdor, The Hasbury; but the main preference is the holiday resort itself, although in one instance the house is dedicated to the courier – Mafalda.

Australia takes Pewsey Vale, Berkshire and Abingdon and in return gives us Billabong, Koala and Strines.

Location

IN THE early part of the century the word 'view' was very popular and there were many houses named Broad View, Meadow View, Field View and similar – indeed the much-loved cartoon strip in a daily newspaper featured Pip, Squeak and Wilfred who lived at Fair View. Today the idea of a view is often conveyed by names such as Panorama, Hillandale and the increasingly popular Bella Vista and Buena Vista which have superseded Bellevue. However 'view' is still used, but sometimes in rather more unusual ways, for example What-a-View and Gorgeous View (which is a clever name as the house overlooks the Avon Gorge). On the other hand Weadavu and No View have come to terms with their particular situations. One Fair View was just that at one time, but unfortunately it now looks straight into a high-rise block of flats. Castle Peep is appropriate.

There is an increasing risk today of being overtaken by development, and The Lone Cottage may indeed have been so half a century ago, but now is nothing of the kind. Alpha and Omega are fine if there is no possibility of houses being tucked in alongside. Finale is a new house sited at the end of a narrow lane between older properties and taking up the last square yard of building land in the road so that should be safe for a few years. Fifty years ago Boundary House was accurately described, but today the borough extends a quarter of a mile or more beyond it.

Some names must cause endless difficulty for delivery people – think of trying to find Back of Beyond or Mono House now anything but alone, and Ways End which adjoins yet another housing estate. Opposite the Ducks and Opposite the Cricketers Arms are quite superb ingenuities – how long will it be before they follow the fate of Turnpike House and Crossing Keeper's Cottage? Cawna Cottage is fairly safe.

Nevertheless some people have managed to find inspiration – Justandy is not solely occupied by Andrew – it is very convenient for shops, buses and the beach. The Other Cottage is most imaginative while there really are only two, but The House on the Left, named more than fifty years ago, had to acquire another name once the builders moved in. Overholme overlooks the owner's family home.

Names indicating height are less vulnerable – Up Top, Top of the Hill, Hill Crest (very popular in the 1930s), Midstars, Steppes (pun appropriate only if the house is completely isolated), The Heights, Topspot. Stepping Down is on a slope, Farther Down is at the bottom of a lane giving on to a river bank, By Bridge is fairly terse, T'Otherside and Up Right depend on where you are standing and Round the Bend could be open to more than one interpretation.

Nature

WHETHER we live in the middle of a town or in a quiet country village, we British love house names with a rural flavour, and especially those derived from trees. Over the years there have been distinct fashions in tree names. The one most frequently used is The Elms, and this name has been in vogue for at least a hundred and fifty years, and has given rise to many variants such as Elmsleigh, Elmside, Barn Elms and similar derivatives. Elms Close has the trees nearby. Elms figure in myths from many parts of the world. Some thought an elm was the first woman.

An elm growing in front of a Swedish home was regarded as the dwelling of the spirit who guarded the family. In the twelfth century those guilty of crimes were 'by the heeles drawn then to The Elmes in Smithfield and there hanged'. Whether people were aware of the significance of the elm or not, well before The Limes, Ashleigh or Oake Dene figured on front doors, Elm Cottage or The Elms was frequently found in any group of named houses. What will happen to the frequency of this name now that many of our elms are disappearing remains to be seen.

The Laurels (symbol of victory and peace, also alleged to have magic powers), The Hollies, The Firs were much in evidence on prosperous middle-class houses with large front gardens full of evergreens, but names like The Beeches and The Cedars have given way to modern variants such as Copper Beeches, Conifers, The Spinney, Silver Birch, Twin Oaks, Cherry Orchard or, currently fashionable, Tree Tops (not always in an elevated position, but sometimes imaginatively illustrated) and High Trees. At one Burnt Oak they have a 400-year old hollow oak where apparently drunks used to be locked up. Woodview, Twixtrees, Autumn Twigs, Fircones, Leaves or Conkers – almost any derivative is acceptable.

Azaleas to Zinnias, Bluebells to the Malayan Ylang Ylang which sounds like a doorbell ringing – think of a flower and someone will have used it as a house name. Hollyhocks, Primrose Nook, Oleander, Edelweiss, Jasmine Cottage, Meadowsweet, Wisteria – there are hundreds of such names. Occasionally an alternative version of the more familiar name is chosen – Buddles (marigolds), Paigles (cowslips) or Mollyblobs (marsh marigolds). Sometimes the flower image is generalised – Flower Patch, Manyflowers. But the favourite flower of all for a house name source is, and always has been, the rose and hundreds of house names are based on it in one form or another, from simply Rose Cottage (often illustrated with a pretty plaque) to more elaborate ones such as Rose Haven, Roselands, Rosecroft, Rosedale, Rosebank and Floribunda.

Some fruits make good house names too – Elderberry End, Plumtree Cottage, Lemon Cottage and apples in dozens of forms – Applegarth, Apple Acre, Apple Orchard and so on. Melon Garden stands on land that once grew melons for the nearby Castle.

Herbs and spices make delightful cottage names – Mint

Mead, Clove Cottage, Saffronfield, Mustard Copse, Nutmeg Cottage and Peppercorns.

When the British are allegedly a nation of animal lovers, it is somewhat surprising to find so few house names dedicated to our domestic pets. There are one or two dogs – The Corgis, Pekescroft, Beaglepoint (where they keep beagles and pointers), Poodleville and Paw Prints, but remarkably few cats and kittens. Teddy Bear Cottage is named after an apricot poodle, Whiskey is also named after the dog, and Romiladon is a blended name which includes the family pet Paddy. Hoofprints appears from time to time; the rather unusual Popham Down turns out to be the name of a race-horse successfully backed. White Horses with a sea view could refer to rough waves, but inland usually denotes horse owners.

With wild animals, however, and particularly native ones, the case is different and there are hundreds from this source to be seen. The badger is very popular – Badgers Holt, Badgers Earth, Badgers Hollow – and so is the fox, usually in the form of Fox Run, Fox Dell, Foxcroft and similar combinations. The squirrel too has a great following – Squirrels Wood, Squirrel Bank, Squirrels Leap. At Little Dragons they discovered a great collection of lizards in their new garden and, of course, Hedgehog House has its resident. In fact, all kinds of animals are to be found – Deer Leap, Beavers Bank, Lizard's Leap, Snail Creep, Frog's Croak, Moles Retreat, Vache View, Toad's Green and Leverets (on Hare Hill). It is not known why L'Elephant was so named; it may possibly be that when it was built it was the largest house in the neighbourhood. Twiga (giraffe) House is owned by people who spent part of their lives in Tanzania where the giraffe was the national emblem. Some people who find the choice too wide, or maybe have a large family or a variety of pets settle for Noah's Ark.

The popularity of bird names as house names is of fairly recent origin, with a few exceptions. The Rookery (usually on large, rather dark houses surrounded by tall trees) has been in use at least since the end of the nineteenth century; and the robin appeared in a few forms in the 1930s – Robinwood, Robinsbank, and still retains a place in such names as Robin's Oak, Robin's Roost, Robin's Hey although the derivative is sometimes a personal name rather than that of the bird. Robin's Return is a piece of music, but in one instance signifies the home of one who spends much of his working week travelling about and returns at the weekend.

Although birds' names are not used as often as those of trees or flowers (there are more on the coast than inland, and here they often relate to gulls – Gulls' Way, Gull Point, Full Cry), today there are many delightful combinations to be seen – Heronwater, Potter's Heron, Owls Hoot, Larkbarrow, Pigeon Point, Cuckoo Bushes, Pheasant's Rise, Eagle's Ledge, Jays Hatch, Swan Acre – even Flamingos, Penguins and Parrots have a place. Magpies (and in one instance, the Latin form Pica Pica) and Woodpeckers (occasionally its green variety – Yaffles) can be found countrywide. Those who could not make up their minds which bird to honour compromised with Warblers End or The Aviary. England does not share France's liking for swallows where Les Hirondelles can be seen climbing up dozens of walls in wrought-iron 'handwriting', usually accompanied by a flight of wrought-iron swallows.

Apart from some delightful Cottages – Cobweb, Moth, Beehive and Honeypot, references to insects are few in the UK, although there is a Cicada in a south London suburb.

The British are renowned for their preoccupation with the weather, and this is borne out by the large number of names connected with the sun and the wind, the two features of the weather that are used most frequently for house names. It is surprising that names suggesting cold and draughts are so very popular – Windy Ridge, Four Winds, Windsmeet, All Wynds, East Winds, Force Ten. The most original 'wind' name found so far is Snuff-the-Wind. Mistral, the wind experienced in the south of France (often associated with periods of frustration and bad temper) is beginning to appear on newly named houses. However, few names come from the rain.

Large, old houses frequently have names like Sunnyside, Sunny Bank or Sunnydale carved into the stonework by the gate, but although these names can be found on modern houses, 'sun' is used in a much wider variety of ways today. Between the wars Sunrays was often accompanied by a sunray design on the wooden entrance gates or on porthole windows of coloured glass. With the coming of post-war picture windows names like Suntrap spread, but now the sun is used in many different forms – Sunpath, Sundown, Sunshine Four Ways, Sun-Up – even Sunrise opposite to Sunset (not to mention Sunset Strip – an isolated rural dwelling down a muddy lane).

The moon – Half Moon, Hunters Moon; the stars – Cassiopeia, Aquila; the seasons – Springtime, Summer Orchard, Autumn Tints, Winter Hill; feasts and festivals – Christmas Pie House, Easter Cottage, Michaelmas Croft, Lammas Cottage, Candlemas; months of the year – April Cottage, May Villa, September House (November and December have little appeal) and days of the week – Friday House, all provide some people with a satisfying house name.

Verbal Contortions

BACKSPELLINGS can halt the passer-by or leave him in total confusion, and this device is gaining in popularity, but it seems to be mainly confined to names of countries and counties – Adanac, Selaw and Llawnroc in particular (apt, of course, for those just returned); personal names that will adapt such as Nostaw, Notwen, Evilo and Revilo; Yadiloh for a cottage by the sea; a few expressions such as Tievoli and Emohym and there is at least one Rood Egats. Some people are following in the footsteps of Dylan Thomas's Welsh village of Llareggub, but the custom had started before he wrote *Under Milk Wood*. The finest of them all was chosen by someone who likes to shut her front door, put the kettle on and put her feet up and her house name expresses her sentiments – Llamedos.

There are other ways of inventing names: the spoonerism – Gorldly Woods for Worldly Goods; the pun – Shilly Chalet; the occasional palindrome such as Noyon, and there are sometimes alarming anagrams such as Telvesno (Love Nest).

Another device which is becoming increasingly fashionable is a name actually made from the number and quite a few of these can be seen in the industrial Midlands. Sometimes the number will be merely 'written' out – Two-o-Four or One Hundred and Five; occasionally a word will have been manufactured – Fortitoo and Ayteen are good examples of this; and further, local speech patterns are taken into account at Wun and Wunfreo (130). Too Be is quite clever.

A house in an Oxfordshire village was built by knocking two cottages No. 11 and No. 12 into one, and the resulting name is Leventwel. Trinity goes one better as here there are three in one.

Plot 39, the original plot number when the site was planned, has now become its proper name.

There is an infinite variety of names using the comic effect of phonetic spelling – Med-o-Vue, Jusrite, Sudden-Lee, and this kind of fearful jollity can frequently be found in seaside areas where holiday homes by the score appear with names such as Jolidays, Hi Jinx, Tyn-y-clogs, Jollywulblow, Tilwen and so on. It is impossible to escape these and there are a number of examples in other sections of this book.

Joy and
Happiness

IT IS obvious from the legends on the nameplates that some people delight in names suggesting a carefree existence, one of peace and security, but will frequently choose a foreign expression or a manufactured word to convey this. Are they afraid to tempt the gods by openly declaring Happy Home? Perhaps such expressions as Pax, Hapinest, Tran Cwility, Merriemakers, Sans Bruit, Dulce Domum and several versions of Wi Wurrie are a form of touching wood. One of the most frequently used expressions in this category is Sans Souci (without care) – the name of the summer residence of Frederick the Great in East Germany. Arcady and Arcadia are often chosen to represent an ideal rustic paradise. There are, of course, straightforward names such as Peaceful Home, Halcyon and several forms of Merry names – Merrydale, Merryfields, Merrymead. Among the favourites in the 1930s were Homestead and versions of Homelea (Holmeleigh, Holmlea), and these were closely followed by The Nook and The Haven.

A new one to appear on the scene in recent years is Charisma – meaning 'star quality'. Whoopee is perhaps not in quite the same vein, but at least it suggests enjoyment.

One owner moved to the West of England not feeling very well, but having found excellent medical treatment and good friends recovered 'as if by magic' and now lives at Magica. New Chapter (with a nameplate in the form of an open book) signified a brand new house for one couple's first home of their own.

Esperanza is usually chosen to mean 'hope'. An Esperanza near Bristol is named after a ship that went down in the Severn as part of the wreckage is supposed to have been brought into the house. Speranza, which is also sometimes seen, could be ironical because of its occurrence in the most famous and forbidding of all inscriptions over doors: *Lasciate ogni speranza, voi ch'entrate* (All hope abandon, ye who enter here) from Dante's *Inferno*. This quotation has always been popular and has been seen over doors everywhere from Shropshire pubs to RAF Nissen huts, so Speranza may well carry convivial associations or memories of Service comradeship.

People

A HUNDRED or more years ago it was often the custom to name a house or a road after a famous person, and there are many roads, houses and cottages named after the great figures of the day – Nelson, Wellington, Blucher, Gordon. In recent years many of our new housing estates have roads dedicated to the great literary figures – Shakespeare, Keats, Wordsworth, Tennyson and so on, but this has had little effect on the names of the houses in them.

The custom of naming modern houses after the great and the good seems to have died out by World War II and nowadays it is only very occasionally that houses will be named after people. One very fine example though is Brunel, located not far from one of Brunel's bridges, with a beautiful sculptured sign in gold leaf. A fitting tribute.

Civic authorities sometimes choose to name blocks of flats after local dignitaries or famous people – Royce Court after Sir Frederick Royce, John F. Kennedy Heights, Churchill House, Macmillan House, Attlee House, Cavell House, Peabody Buildings (after George Peabody who gave £2½ million in the mid-nineteenth century to the City of London for the construction of low rental working men's tenements), Nuffield House, Browning Towers – there are many such examples throughout the country. The story behind Fletcher Court and Hambrook Court in London is an interesting one. An unexploded bomb was found in Camden and defused by the Army's Bomb Disposal Squad: later the then Borough Council very fittingly named two blocks of dwellings after the soldiers involved.

Occasionally properties will be known by the names of the people who originally built or owned them – Copes Cottages, Blake House, Palmers, Beechams Cottages – these are a few examples of dwellings that have retained, or whose new owners have revived, their original names. In a few instances newcomers give a house a new name, but the locals will go on referring to it as Greyson's Tenement in spite of a smart sign announcing Meadowvale on its front gate.

Jobs

IN YEARS past dwellings that went with jobs were frequently cottages, each belonging to a specific occupation – Groom's Cottage, Shepherd's Cottage, Potter's Cottage. Today many of these old names are being revived by new owners who take a pride in living at The Saddlers, Weavers, The Old Bakehouse, The Gloving – or even The Old Seven Stars or The King's Head, former public houses now turned into private dwellings.

Until very recently there were very few modern houses named after their owners' occupations. Gasworks Cottage and Tramway Lodge were functional in the 1930s, and the Services produced a few – Admiral's Rest, Mariners, Sailor Cottage. Occupations such as draughtsman, fitter or shorthand typist do not readily lend themselves to house names. However, in the past year or two there has been a noticeable change in fashion in this area, and now there are a number of houses reflecting the owners' jobs: Sparksville and Megohm (owned by electricians); Choppers (a helicopter designer); Blades (a helicopter pilot); Crochet

Rest (a piano tuner); Welder's Lodge; Boffins (a scientist); Top Gear (a driving instructor). A doctor lives at Bedside Manor and Izzy Inn is the home of a handyman whose neighbours are constantly ringing his door bell and demanding of his wife 'Is he in? My tap is leaking'. Seldom Inn is in a slightly different vein. Coppers End is rather clever – the house was once a police station and also the owner uses copper in his business. Coppers View overlooks a row of police houses. Shop House was once a shop. Goldcrest has been named by a Royal Naval Officer after the Royal Naval Air Station in South Wales, and another naval one is Boatswains, complete with nautical illustrations.

Kiddlewink was a seine loft for the pilchard fishermen of Cornwall. Traphole is both unusual and apt, as fishermen used to set traps for fish in the river immediately outside the house.

Someone in the paper business chose Saqquara, the name of one of the most important archaeological sites in Egypt, because some of the best examples of early writings on papyrus were found there.

Stage Door is owned by a professional actor and collector of theatrical miscellanea. He has the stage door keeper's collection of signed photographs of artists who appeared at the Princes Theatre, Bristol, from 1890 to 1910, and among other interesting items, a letter from the owner of the dog on the HMV label.

Retirement

RETIREMENT for some people means a move –
often to the coast or to a beauty spot such as the Lake
District or the Dales, and whilst they may be glad to leave
behind them the noise and bustle of the cities and the
demands of jobs, yet many are reluctant to sever entirely
their former way of life and so areas much sought after for
retirement such as England's south coast abound with
names like Barnsley, Sydenham, Durham, Hainault and
Cheam, and many a pretty Cornish village has a Wakefield,
Perivale or Croydon.

Former occupations are recalled at Dunbakin, Duty Dun
(a retired policeman), Chocksin (a former Fleet Air Arm
Officer), Abadan House (whose owner once worked in the
oilfields of the Middle East), Admiral's Rest and Bowling
Over (a retired cricketer).

Dunroamin and Dunrovin are ubiquitous, but their
derivatives Dunhuntin, Dunlukin and Dunmovin have never
enjoyed such popularity Stayinholm, Settledown, The Moor-

ings, Gone to Ground, Journey's End, Chez Dernier, Cottage of Content, Restholme and Hove To are just a few of the names chosen by the retired.

Outspan – rather a clever way of indicating that the yoke or harness of responsibility has been dropped – is appearing much more frequently in recent years.

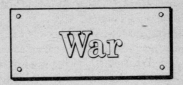

War

IN THE early nineteenth century when, for some, war was a gentlemanly business, conjuring up pictures of famous generals and daring battles, it was fashionable to call your house something like Trafalgar House, Wellington Villa, Blucher Lodge or Nelson Cottage. As the years went by grim reminders of Mafeking, Balaklava, Spion Kop, Ladysmith and Omdurman appeared both as house names and street names. By the end of World War II very few houses bore military names – one or two remained from the First World War like Anzac and Zeppelin, and although two narrow boats were called Montgomery and Wavell, war was too close to need further reminders. In fact, the name of one house, Belsen had to be changed. A characteristic sidelight did however occur in Cardiff during the blitz. The house next door to Mon Abri was hit by a bomb and the following morning it bore a sign saying Mon Debris.

References to war have not disappeared entirely from our gateposts, but today they tend to be reminders from history – Cromwell Cottage, Boscobel, and in places near the site where battles took place you will find Culloden, Naseby, Senlac and Sedgemoor. The village of Cropredy in Oxfordshire does not forget that in June 1644 the Parliamentarians under Waller were defeated by the Royalists under Charles I. A row of cottages was erected in 1899 and each has a name incised to commemorate the event – Waller, Kentish, Culverin, Cavalier, Cleveland and Charles – all followed by the word 'Cottage'.

Retired Service personnel sometimes choose regimental mottoes or other reminders of their military careers, so one occasionally sees Per Ardua, Fidelis, Sappers or Greenjackets, and three men stationed in Safaga, Egypt, during World War II each determined to buy a house and name it Safaga once they had reached home safely – one at least did just that. Chindit House was owned by someone with connections with General Wingate and the Burma Star Association, and Derna is a reminder of military service in Libya.

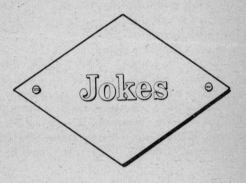

Jokes

J OKE names have existed since the nineteenth century, but no earlier period has seen anything like their enormous popularity today.

There are plenty of people around who choose names like Hangovers, Gone to Ground, The Last Straw (appropriate enough when it is the last thatched cottage in a row), Byatube next to Soarewe, Chez Wen next door to Chez Nous, Beanto (one wonders where), Dunbuzin, The Bolt Hole, Moonrakers, and Manna (a totally unexpected gift). Working Class is intended to be the name of a house where ducks are kept in the back yard since, according to a recent book on social class, the aristocracy shoot ducks, the middle class have china flights of them on their lounge walls (they did at one time, but I have not seen many recently) and the working class keep them in their back yards.

Two adjacent old houses provide what must surely be an unintentional joke – Tor Down next to Moor View.

Literature

IF YOU think of Waverley, Kenilworth and Ivanhoe you begin to imagine the names carved into tall grey stone pillars, perhaps surmounted by a globe or an acorn. Behind the front walls will be laurels and the houses will be the imposing suburban residences of the early part of our present century when no bookshelf was complete without a set of the *Waverley Novels*. Ivanhoe was the most popular name from Scott and is found on houses all over the world; Waverley and Kenilworth were strong runners up. Marmion and Lochinvar are still on a few older houses, in leaded fanlights or carved grey stone, over front doors opening on porches with patterned tiled floors and cast iron umbrella stands.

The habit of using literature as a source of house names is a sporadic and comparatively modern one. Changes in popular taste seem to have influenced it much more than the growth of secondary education. The vogue for Scott affected house names at the turn of the century but our other literary examples are more recent, even when they are drawn from writers earlier than Scott.

In 1933 James Hilton's novel *Lost Horizon* appeared. It was to be filmed: it was broadcast on the new wireless sets of the suburban 1930s and it gave the world a name that still means peace and seclusion in a timeless Himalayan retreat. Shangri-la is one of the most popular – and perhaps deservedly popular – house names of all time, and Shangri-la nameplates in all shapes and sizes are still appearing on houses throughout the world. In one instance the name was chosen after the house escaped bombing in World War II.

By comparison Erewhon from Samuel Butler's Utopian novel is only rarely commemorated, though there would be an understandable reluctance to imply that your house was Nowhere.

One somewhat astonishing literary reference is Jalna from the Whiteoaks series by Mazo de la Roche. In nearly every town one finds at least one house, and sometimes several, called Jalna. Why should this one name among the thousands available from literature have been chosen by so many people? Jalna itself was named after the military station in India where Adeline and Philip Whiteoak met and married, but the fictitious house was not even located in England. It would have been much more easy to understand had there been a rash of houses called The Shieling when this was regularly featured in *Mrs Dale's Diary*, but this was not the case.

Manderley (from Daphne du Maurier's *Rebecca*) is a frequent choice and Cranford, Middlemarch, Northanger, Limberlost (from the *Girl of the Limberlost* by Gene Stratton Porter) and Herries from the series by Hugh Walpole turn up occasionally; there is at least one house called Sartor Resartus (from the book by Carlyle), and until recently one named The Case Is Altered from the comedy by Ben Jonson, produced in 1599.

Next door neighbours in Oxfordshire have called their houses Larkrise and Candleford.

But fashions are changing and today's new house namers are turning in large numbers to *The Lord of the Rings* for The Hobbit, Rivendell (frequently to be found in black lettering on a luminous silver background), Bag End (home of Bilbo Baggins), Baggins End and possibly Brandywine (see page 91). *The Wind in the Willows* is now providing more names too, with houses actually called The Wind in the Willows, Mole End and Toad Hall, and there are increasing numbers of The House at Pooh Corner, Just Pooh, Eeyores Place, The Wolery and Trespassers W–. Lear readers have come up with Chankly Bore and Coromandel (where lived the Yonghi Bonghi Bo – although there is the Coromandel Range of mountains in New Zealand and it is also a type of wood).

Shakespearian references do not turn up as often as might have been expected. There are Elsinore, Cymbeline, Oberon, John O'Gaunt's, Cressida and a few Hamlets in Britain, and a Dunsinane in Jamaica.

Greenmantle, Lilliput, Pookshill, Lodore and Stella Maris put in brief appearances (although one house named Stella Maris commemorates the ship that played such an important part in the relief of Malta during World War II). Gunga Din was a pre-war choice, but this particular one has now vanished and I have not noticed any others of that name in my travels. Lift the Latch came directly from a 1910 novel and has been retained through a change of ownership. A most appropriate name provided it is not taken literally by unwanted callers. It is inscribed on a bell with a clapper.

Dickens has been responsible in years past for both house and road names, and a number of people have chosen

Copperfield and Bleak House, although one person con-
fessed she was always waiting for something to turn up and
hence named her house Micawber. There is at least one
Dotheboys Hall.

Seagulls Cry is on the Cornish coast, but its name is not
derived from the calling gulls that constantly fly overhead. It
came from the title of the novel *Seagulls Cry* by Denise
Robins who actually stayed in the house while writing the
book.

Pantomime

IT IS quite remarkable how one book, one musical or one film will inspire vast numbers of house namers leaving the rest to have, at the most, an occasional mention, but in general to be totally ignored. So it is with pantomime where Cinderella is one of very few characters to be remembered. She turns up both in this country and on the Continent and one owner has named all her houses Cinderella. She first started with Cinderella Cottage, then moved to a bigger property and called it Cinderella House. Now she lives in greater style at Cinderella Lodge and is hoping one day to acquire Cinderella Castle.

Another, but infrequent, pantomime reference is Peter Pan and this is found occasionally at the seaside on holiday houses – with Wendy next door in some places. Harlequin (or Harlequins) turns up occasionally, but sometimes this just indicates that there are multi-coloured panels on the front door.

Music

IN SPITE of transistors, record players and the ever-present background music, music cannot be said to be a major source of inspiration to house owners. Until recently musical names tended to come from musical shows – Kismet, Salad Days, Carousel and one which is almost as popular as Jalna and can be found in pretty nearly every part of the country – Bali Hai from the enormously successful show South Pacific. Most of these are reminders of enjoyable evenings, first dates or shows seen on honeymoons. One, however, was chosen on the spur of the moment. A solicitor was dealing with the legal aspects of a house purchase and remarked to his clients that if they did not choose a name quickly the property would soon be dubbed

'The New Bungalow'. Somewhat at a loss for a suitable name, they spied a poster advertising the show South Pacific, and Bali Hai solved their problem. Romantic links with the past are also forged by Tralee, Rose Marie and Vienna Woods.

There are a few classical reminders – Solveig, Faust Lodge, Campanella, Glyndebourne, Karelia; an occasional Mozart and Haydn; Gilbert and Sullivan fans usually go for Tit Willow, but outnumbering all the musical references put together is Greensleeves. It appears throughout the country in a variety of styles and lettering on all kinds of houses from large to small. It serves several purposes. Not only do most people know the tune, but it is a reminder of a bygone era which some people fondly imagine to have been idyllically rural and simple.

Contrabasso was named by a double bass player. General musical terms are sometimes used, such as Melody and Rhapsody, and sometimes terms like Duet or Quintet indicate the size of family.

But the pop world is encroaching, and already there are Half a Sixpence and Shiralee inspired by Tommy Steele; Artizan after a pop group run by the son of the house, and although Atlantic Crossing is actually on the North Cornwall coast, it is taken from the name of a Rod Stewart album.

However, one of the cleverest musical references can be found on some French homes – a treble clef with the notes Doh Mi Si La Doh Ray (domicile adoré). The nearest thing to this found so far in the United Kingdom is a house with double gates and on each in wrought iron is the line of music 'There's no place like home'.

Media

Television, Radio, Newspapers and Films

THE Canadian sage Marshall McLuhan described the modern world as 'an electronic village'. At least some of the house names in the electronic village show the varying influences of television. Others originate in radio programmes, films or newspaper features.

One of the first house names to be derived from a TV serial was Ponderosa and this is sometimes decorated with a set of horns (and sometimes it is misspelled too). This was quickly followed by Daktari, Tardis, Emmerdale, Tannoch Brae, Robin Hill (sometimes, but not always, inspired by the *Forsyte Saga*), Kes and Alvega (the Dalek Planet of the Intelligent Plants). The village of Marsh had, of course, to have a house called Much Binding, but the many houses now called Panorama usually have extensive views and this name has taken over from the popular Fair View of the 1930s.

Ken Dodd's Knotty Ash has, indirectly, become associated with a house in Somerset. Originally the house was called Knotty Ash because there was a very large ash tree in the garden which was difficult to fell on account of the knots in it. However, on outings from their plastics factory, some people with a lovely sense of humour have deposited a number of 'Diddy' people on the doorstep and so the name has acquired slightly different overtones.

One very recent phenomenon must be noted here and that is a house name from a strip cartoon. Snoopy has gained such tremendous international popularity that I suppose it was inevitable that someone should name a house Peanuts (and better still that the next owner should not only retain the name but add an illustration to the nameplate).

Films seem to inspire people less than books, but a very popular name seen all over the country is Tara from the name of Scarlett O'Hara's house in *Gone With the Wind* (although Tara is also a place name and, for some, it could be a reference to Thomas Moore's ballad that begins 'The harp that once through Tara's halls ...'). Sayonara is allegedly Japanese for a kind of farewell such as 'Au revoir', 'Until we meet again' and this was chosen for one house through a film starring John Wayne in which he used this expression. Shiralee comes from a Tommy Steele film, but this is also thought to derive from an Australian Aboriginal source meaning 'the taking on of responsibility' – an appropriate choice for householders with a mortgage. Sundance could have a dual reference – the film and the weather.

Sports
and Hobbies

PRACTICALLY every aspect of life imaginable con-
tributes in some way to the naming of a house and as most
people have a hobby of some kind it is only to be expected
that there will be many house names reflecting the interests
of the occupiers. This is particularly noticeable near golf
clubs – especially those near the coast where many
members have probably retired and chosen to live in that
spot on account of a first-class course. Hence not only will
the fairly obvious references be found – The Links, Linksyde,
The Tees and Bunkers, but a few more unusual ones such as
Mashie Niblick and Pin High.

There can be few people who are not aware of the impact
of football, but only an occasional name bears any reference
to any of its forms, perhaps because so many of its

supporters do not, as yet, own houses. Nevertheless, real devotees (or sometimes parents indulging their children) choose Anfield, Chelsea, Home Ground (quite clever, this) and Scrummage, which could also relate to several aspects of family life.

Those whose real joy in life is motoring, are more willing to proclaim their interests with names such as Carmania. The Pits belongs to motor racing enthusiasts as their concreted front garden resembled racing pits when all their friends gathered before a big event. Tee Ar Too, Classic and Lagonda commemorate particular makes of car. Bunnies Leap (although it has a picture of rabbits in the hall) is really named after a hill-climb and Silverstone needs no explanation. Peak Revs is most unusual – here the son of the owner built a car and eventually succeeded in getting it into peak condition while he lived in the house.

From cricket comes Owzatt, Sticky Wicket and Wickets located behind The Bat and Ball (once a pub). Dunbowlin and Bowling Over belong to retired cricketers. Keen sailors have chosen The Wrigglers (the name of rocks off Falmouth), Sails, Spinnaker, Slipways and Sailcote.

Although Ludo and Snakes and Ladders have not, as yet, been found, at least one house is dedicated to Mah Jong.

If you are fortunate enough to live in a converted railway station then you have a ready made name – Loddiswell Station. On the other hand you may collect railway memorabilia and hang old signs such as Reading General above your door. Essandee is on the side of the track of the old Somerset and Dorset Light Railway. Fiferails was built by former railway people from Fife and the original sign was on a piece of wood that was once part of the track. At Puffers they are keen on model railways (and also live near a main line), but Puffers Cottage has nothing whatsoever to do with trains – its former owner was a bit short of breath!

A Clarence is a four-wheeled private carriage and some people who moved to Clarence Road (doubtless named for other reasons) had the brilliant idea of linking their house name with the name of the road in a rather unusual way. They came up with Shandrydan – a light two-wheeled cart. Phaeton is named after yet another form of old-fashioned transport – a four wheeled open carriage usually drawn by a pair of horses.

At Valetta is an expert in topiary who has a topiary hedge of the destroyer HMS Valetta.

Popular

THERE are no real demarcations in types of names in various parts of the country, but it is noticeable that for some reason certain names do seem to be more popular in some areas. For example, Tamarisk is a firm favourite in South West Devon and Cornwall; Greystones abounds in Somerset; The White House is well liked in Hampshire; names with 'rose' in them occur frequently in Gloucestershire. Around the turn of the century, Walsall, in the industrial Midlands, had a liking for names connected with trees or ferns. The suffix '-royd' occurs frequently on houses in the north (but not exclusively so).

In the first half of the nineteenth century houses of middle class prosperous business people usually had words such as 'House' 'Villa' 'Lodge' or 'Cottage' after the name – Grosvenor House, Sussex Villa, Woodbine Lodge, Bath Cottage. Later in the century names of trees became fashionable, usually preceded by 'The' – The Beeches, The Firs, The Hawthorns, The Hollies – and their large front gardens had trees to match. By 1900 the single name had become fashionable. Grand names like Clarence House or Oxford Villa did not go with very small houses and so Villa became '-ville' and Roseville, Larchville, Ethelville and scores of similar names made their appearance. Whereas The Ferns or Fern Hill belonged to the larger type of house built in the 1880s, this was the era of Fernleigh, Fernhurst and Ferndale.

In the period between the two world wars, thousands of houses were built and named, and the patterns of naming changed again. Many were straightforward and domestic and fairly typical are Wayside, Byways, Homelea, Hazeldene, Glenthorne and Oakhurst. Many were named after beauty spots in Britain – Windermere and Jesmondene; many after personal names fashionable at the time – Maryville and Maydene.

Radical changes have taken place since the end of World War II, and this era of social revolution and the permissive society is reflected in names displayed (and sometimes flaunted) on houses. Names come from all over the world; they appear in many languages to astound and delight the passer-by. It is no longer the age of Waverley, The Laurels and Homestead, but of Karenza, Costaplenti, Maurob, Casanova, Jusrite and Llamedos.

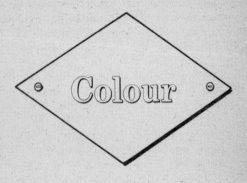

Colour

HOUSE names using colours have been in fashion for over a hundred years. The colour most often chosen is green which is what would be expected in view of the literary and mythological significance 'green' has had from the earliest times. The colour has always carried associations of pastoral peace and of harmony with the underlying forces of nature as in Marvell's ' . . . *a green thought in a green shade*'. It is not, for obvious reasons, used on its own as in The White House or The Red House, but combined with another name – generally based on nature – such as Green Leaves, Green Lawns, Green Banks, Green Meadows and similar. The second favourite colour is grey – again combined with another word, and here the most frequently chosen combination is Greystones, which far exceeds other 'grey' names such as Grey Gables or Greylands. Silver has its followers – Silverdene, Silvercombe; a few choose blue – Blue Door, Blue Hills; red usually refers to a feature of the building – Red Roof, Red Tyles, Red Dormers and, with very few exceptions, the remainder are white (even though the house may now be painted pink or yellow) – Whitecroft, White Haven, White Gables or, the most popular, just The White House or The White Cottage.

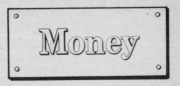

Money

WHEN it comes to talking of money we, as a nation, are nowhere near as reticent as we used to be. At one time it was unthinkable to infer you could not afford to buy something; now it seems quite permissible to announce to the world on your gatepost Stilowin, Long Loan, Costaplenti, Beam Ends (although this can have another meaning), Stoney Broke – or perhaps with an air of pride, Dunowin or Paide. Sometimes, of course, such names are chosen in defiance, for example, one householder displays Costa Brava and, not to be outdone, his neighbour declares Costa Fortune. One Costalot got its name when the owners were laying out the garden entirely in flagstones and a passer-by remarked 'I expect that cost a lot'. In similar vein Farthings, Pennies or Coppers can indicate the state of the householder's bank balance once the deposit had been found. (One Coppers Close, however, refers to a nearby police station.) At Fort Knox they were fed up with gloomy prophesying by relatives that they would find it hard to pay the mortgage.

One couple who liked to have everything worked out properly before embarking on undertakings, particularly large scale ones such as buying a house, were considering all the pros and cons of their proposed new home when she remarked 'This is a bit of a shaky do'. But it all worked out satisfactorily and they now live at Shaky Doo.

JEWELLERY plays little part in house naming. Ruby Cottage was named nearly a hundred years ago and could have been taken from a personal name. Occasionally names like Gemdene, Topaz and Koh-i-Noor can be seen. Kimberley is popular, but for a variety of reasons – at least one person felt she was investing in what she hoped would turn out to be her own little diamond mine. Zircon was named after the stone in the owner's engagement ring.

France

THE French, who pride themselves on their Gallic
wit and their devotion to all household things, might be
expected to produce their own varieties and vintages of
house names – a sort of Appellations peu Contrôlées.
Wrought iron calligraphy adorns the gleaming white or
tawny brown stucco favoured in the new housing developments of suburban fringes or the Mediterranean littoral.
High on the list is Les Hirondelles, more often than not
accompanied by a flight of wrought iron swallows. Here, too,
are bars of music (see page 56) which tell the passer-by that
the house is much loved. Chez Nous and Mon Repos will be
found, but among the favourites are Mon Rêve or Notre
Rêve (Our Dream) with Le Nid (The Nest) not far behind. In
the south in particular the sun provides many names – Clair
Soleil, Face Au Soleil. Humorous names occur here perhaps
more than in Spain or Portugal with ones such as Panique,
El E Nou, Cha Noo, Ma-Guy, Mon P'tit Ami and Et Voilà
(doubtless the equivalent of the English Tiz Yer). The idea of
a welcome can frequently be seen in a name such as Au Bon

Accueil. Les Palmiers (The Palms) are much in evidence, and in Provence there is a wealth of names in Provencal. Here much is made of the ever-present cricket and there are some attractive nameplates portraying Les Cigales. Some modern houses are either designed like windmills or else are converted old windmills and so Moulin often figures in the name – Moulin des Baumes.

The universal word 'Villa' is often employed – Villa Mon Desir, Villa Bleue. Girls' names are used occasionally – Marie, Jeanne, Mireille and Odette, and the modern device of using initials – Les Deux J.

Small rural villages which have not developed have very few names – they rely on numbers, traditionally white on a blue enamelled plate. The majority of French house names are to be found either on properties out in the country and just off the main road when a large board with a collection of names can be seen on the side of the road indicating a group of houses nearby, or else on the new bungalows on the outskirts of towns or other new developments.

Occasionally a house name will be used imaginatively; for instance, Les Marguerites has a very deep but delicate frieze of white marguerites on a pale blue background right across the front of an attractive old town house in the foothills of the Pyrenees.

It is most interesting to note that whereas we are very keen to label our houses Menton, Biarritz or San Tropez, there does not seem to be an equivalent enthusiasm for French houses to be called Scarborough, Polperro or Windermere. There is, however, a two-way traffic; we borrow Mon Repos, Chez Nous and Bonne Nuit and lend them English or Franglais names such as At Home, My Home, Mary-Jack – even Les Bungalows.

Spain and Portugal

THE Iberian Peninsula has some of the most interesting and beautiful name plates to be found anywhere. Many are ceramic and take the form of a large plaque in white with a blue decorative border.

In general, house names are urban and suburban (one in fact in Spain is actually called Villa Urbana) rather than rural and in places such as Estoril, Portugal, where there are some magnificent houses belonging to royalty, aristocrats and wealthy business people, as well as the more ordinary seaside dwellings, there are some remarkable names to be seen displayed in truly grand style.

Smaller houses on the coast in Portugal tend to have girls' names, Rose, Mimi, Emma and Carol, often standing on their own, but sometimes preceded by the word Vivenda (meaning home or dwelling) – Vivenda Joaquina, Vivenda Isabel – even Vivenda Nirvana. Sometimes Chalet or Casa will be used instead – Chalet Juliette, Casa Mimosas, Casa Das Flores. Flowers, of course, grow in abundance and so there are very many house names based on flowers.

Many names though are of religious origin, and often there will be some kind of votive device, perhaps a lamp, or a ceramic plaque of the Virgin Mary, over the doorway and the house will have a name like A Luz do Mundo, Vivenda Luzdivina, or Casa de Nostra Senhora da Visitacao. Saints' names abound, but with complete simplicity and naturalness.

Along the coastal belt of Spain thousands of houses are being built and there is a wealth of house names to be found. Although, as with Portugal, there are similar categories of names to those found in Britain, there seem to be fewer humorous names and certainly not so many manufactured ones like Ourouse or Ducumin. Instead of the Portuguese Vivenda, Spain uses Villa or Finca (meaning property) – hence Finca Maria, Villa Pax, Villa Esperanza. One even finds a complete mixture – Finca Blake. Again, many names have religious connections, La Concepcion, but El Pilar is the favourite. This refers to the famous statue of the Virgin Mary on the altar of the great cathedral of pilgrimage in Zaragoza – Nuestra Senora del Pilar. El Pilar can be found on houses throughout Spain. Some houses have names of trees – Los Pinos (pines), Los Chopos (poplars) and Los Cedros (cedars), but vast areas are arid and summers are extremely hot and so Las Palmeras (palms) are only to be expected. Names involving windmills are also found – Molino de Lydia. Quite unexpectedly one then comes across a name like Trinidad.

Le Nid (The Nest) much loved in France but only found

infrequently in Britain, occurs as El Nido, sometimes in what has become an almost universal form of name plate – wrought iron 'handwriting' (usually extremely difficult to see from the road). One El Nido has a wrought iron stork on its front wall, a device few English housewives would readily risk.

If there is a collection of houses up a private road, then often near the entrance will be a wall of ceramic plaques detailing the names of all the houses (and sometimes the owners' names as well).

Quite the most enchanting of all Spanish house names is Los Patos (The Ducks) found on a large house on the outskirts of Madrid. It consists of three wrought iron ducks on the wall near the front entrance gates and each has a name – Julieta, Jaimito and Victoria – presumably the children of the family.

Where house names exist in Spain and Portugal they show variety and charm, both in the choice of names and the way in which they are displayed. Decorative ceramic wall panels, plaques, ornamental lights, even oil paintings in niches, all add to the flair displayed in the style of many of the houses themselves.

Other European Names

HOUSE names are to be found in most parts of the European Continent. In Czechoslovakia there are a number of fine examples on older houses of the kinds of house names that used to be in vogue in the first half of the century. Tabor, Southern Bohemia, has, for example, Vlasta, Slavia, Villa Maruse, Bellevue and Chodska.

There are a wealth of interesting names to be found in Italy, particularly on villas such as the Villa d'Este, named from its owner Cardinal Ippolitto II d'Este, where Liszt was inspired by its Bernini fountain to write a splendid piano piece. Casino Degli Spiriti, where smart Venetian society once met, acquired a decidedly eerie history. It is supposed to have been used as a repository for corpses; there were tales of smuggling, and ghostly associations still cling. Beneath the waters of the Adriatic lies The House of the Seven Dead Men, a name which was acquired through a joke that misfired. According to the local story, some fishermen found a body and took it home. They instructed a young lad to wake the 'visitor' up and bring him in to dinner. This he apparently did, but when the corpse appeared at table all seven fishermen are supposed to have died of fright.

Belgium has a mixture of French and Flemish names – De Groene Man (The Green Man), Ons Huis (Our Home), Het Zonnig Oord (The Sunny Spot), t'Rietenhof (The Reedgarden), De Golven (Waves), Ter Poel (At the Pond), t'Hautland (Woodland) and Vogelsang (Bird's Song) and then names which look much more familiar to us as they are common to many European countries – Belle-Vue, Beau Sejour, Marie-Jose, Dominique and the ubiquitous Le Nid (The Nest).

Switzerland has an abundance of modern houses with names such as Chalet Astrid, Les Pierrettes, Le Mirador, Villa Favorita and Casa Peschiera, but also many whose names are associated with great figures or events from history. Gibbon has several connections with Swiss houses. He wrote *The Decline and Fall of the Roman Empire* at La Grotte, Lausanne, and saw Voltaire act in his own plays at the eighteenth century house known as Mon Repos in Lausanne. Voltaire spent part of several winters at Les Delices, Geneva, and then went to live for a short time at the Chateau Prangins, Lake Geneva. Later this was the home of Joseph Bonaparte. Wagner lived at Villa Wesendonck, Zurich, for a year or so and completed *die Meistersinger* at the Haus Mariafeld. Maison de Verre was built by Le Corbusier in Geneva and Sir Winston Churchill spent his first post-war holiday in 1946 at Villa Choisi.

In the Netherlands, among many names not readily recognisable such as Zonzijde (Sunnyside), Welgelegen (Well situated), Nooitgedacht (never thought of), Weltevrêe (Satisfied), Parkzicht (Park View) and Zeelust (Sea Delight), Ons Nest (Our Nest) pops up again.

Special Foreign Houses

MANY readers of this book will know the Casa de Pilatos in Seville. They will have walked round its spacious main courtyard and admired its graceful columns and heard the legend that this house is so named because it follows the plan of Pontius Pilate's house in Jerusalem.

The Kojumdzioglu House in Plovdiv, Bulgaria, built by Hajji Georgi of Constantinople in 1847, is so called because it once belonged to Argir Kojumdzioglu. It is worth going to Plovdiv just to see this enchanting bow fronted house, built, so the story goes, in the shape of the traditional yoke used for cattle. It now houses an ethnographic museum. Georgi also built another very fine house in Plovdiv, Georgiadi House, now a museum.

Sarospatak in Hungary was fortified and has a fighting floor. It is not a name that would be expected to encourage imitators, though some of those happy suburban families whose homes have acquired unplanned fighting floors of their own might find it appropriate.

In Salamanca, Spain, the House of Shells is famous because of the pattern of carved shells on its exterior, so dramatic in the clear Spanish sunlight and so familiar from a thousand photographs.

But the place of honour in this group must go to a fine sixteenth century house in Narbonne, France, with a certain Renaissance window overlooking a narrow street in the old part of the city. The three caryatids in the central section of the window have kept their architectural page three 'in the sun' since 1558. Because of them, Narbonnais humour has long known the house as the Maison des Trois Nourrices – the House of the Three Wet Nurses.

Foreign Languages

THERE are, of course, hundreds of house names taken from other languages, but some seem to occur time and time again. Right at the top of the list is Cartref, found in practically every town and village and Welsh for 'home'. This is closely followed by Karenza – which is Cornish and means literally 'love, charity, affection', although it is sometimes used as an adaptation of the currently fashionable girl's name Karen. Names from the Maori language have an appeal, particularly for people with New Zealand connections – Tauranga (bay of plenty), Kamaka (stony place); and home owners from Australia sometimes choose the Australian Aboriginal Carinya (happy home). From Swahili come Kaziyetu ('our work' – on a house actually built by its owners) and Inshallah ('God willing'). Kyalami (my home) is believed to be from a Zulu dialect.

In Cornwall, as may well be expected, there are vast numbers of houses with Cornish names, and some of these have spread throughout the country as people have enjoyed holidays in Cornwall, been fascinated by the strange looking names and brought them back as holiday memories. Many are attractive, but errors can be made and great care is needed or you will end up with a name you did not bargain for. For example, Langarth is either used as a transferred place name or is intended to imply 'an enclosed space with a garden' but Lan is really 'enclosed cemetery'; The Fougou is used in the sense of 'retreat' but a fougou is an artificial cave or underground chamber and is a common archaeological feature in West Cornwall, although its purpose is unknown. Some names are quite picturesque – Chy-an-Dour (house by the water); Chybean (little house); Chy Gwyn (white house); Chy-an-Grouse (the house of the cross – in the sense of a monument); Chynance (house in a valley).

There are some ingenious borrowings from many languages. Tighna Dris 'the house of the thorn' has been used on a house owned by some people named Thorne; Nonum is the ninth house in the road; Tir Na Og is Land of Eternal Youth, and Haere Ra has been chosen to imply 'now is the hour'.

The Isle of Man has some splendid examples of delightful names from the Manx language: Loughen-E-Yeigh (pond of the geese); Cronk My Chree (hill of my heart); Creg Dy Shee (rock of peace) and Yn-Cooill (the nook).

If you want a name from another language it is worth checking with someone who knows the language well that you have not unwittingly chosen an unfortunate name. Ty in Welsh means 'house' and thus Ty Coch is Red House and Ty Perllan is Orchard House, but although 'bach' means 'little',

Ty Bach has become a mild vulgarity for 'toilet'. In a similar vein, a family manufacturing a house name from personal names, Henijo, have ended up with a word that bears some similarity to the Japanese for 'public convenience'! Pymp Gwely (intended as Welsh for 'five beds') should really be Pump Gwely. La Mer was chosen, but when La Merde was inscribed on the nameplate it had to be removed rather quickly.

Certain areas of the country at one time attracted retired Service personnel and some, particularly those who had seen service in India, brought back reminders of their overseas postings. In the nineteenth century, Cheltenham had both Malcolm Ghur ('ghur' – house) and Mosquito Ghur, both now gone, but Chota Koti (little house) is still very much in evidence in many parts of the country.

Two French names are international. In the UK Mon Repos and Chez Nous were very popular in the 1930s when wholesale development of private housing took place, making it possible for thousands of people to buy a house of their own, whereas their parents had probably had to make do with a rented house. Thus the names symbolised the fulfilment of ambition. Many examples of these names still remain (particularly Chez Nous – even one version in Hindustani), but they do not now enjoy the enormous popularity that they once did. One family moved from Jersey to Cornwall and when they came to lay out their garden they found large numbers of frogs. As they also had a well they combined both and chose the unusual name of Puits des Grenouilles.

The borrowing from other languages is not purely one-sided. On the Continent you are quite likely to find At Home and Mary-Jack in France; Pin Up and Shangri La in Spain, and Portugal even has its own translation of Mon Repos (Meu Repouso) near Estoril.

The fact that a house name in another language might be difficult both to pronounce and spell is no deterrent. Tzitzikama, Nkokonjeru, Scheherazade and Buakonikani stare defiantly at the postman – goodness knows what they sound like over the telephone.

Certain words from other languages, or languages now dead, have been adopted as part of house names. In particular words implying shelter are fairly common and so houses are called The Bield, The Shieling, The Bothy and occasionally The Humpy and The Borie.

Old terms for small areas of land are sometimes revived – The Pightle, The Croft (with dozens of variants such as Fircroft, Rosecroft, Elmcroft and so on). In the north a favourite suffix is '-royd' (clearing) and there are many names such as Woodroyd, Fernroyd, Holmeroyd, Glenroyd. Garth (garden, paddock, yard) can be seen countrywide, either as The Garth or as a prefix or suffix – Garthside, Rosegarth. Of the hundreds of names ending with '-dene' (vale), by far the most popular is Hazeldene, at its peak in the 1930s, but there are dozens of combinations – Oakdene, Ashdene, Thorndene, Glendene. Leaze (pasture) or Leigh, Lee, Lea are useful and can be combined with a number of other words to form suitable names. In the 1920s and 30s Holmleigh was often chosen, but this is nowhere near so popular today.

Then there are those names which suit some people but infuriate others – Twa Lums (two chimneys) Oor Hoose, Our Ain Hame, Wurain (our own).

With the coming of the package tour expressions from a wide variety of languages have begun to appear on gateposts. Fair View is rapidly being replaced by expressions such as Buena Vista and Bella Vista; Homeleigh by Casa Mia; practically no-one chooses The New House any longer but a number go for Casanova (hard luck on the man about the house); Nuventure is being overtaken by expressions such as Adelante (Spanish – forward) and Sleepy Hollow by Bonne Nuit. Che Sera Sera suggests a very placid home.

Holy Names and Sacred Places

ALONG with the wishes for good fortune, or the deliberate invocations of supernatural powers, come dedications to saints. The idea of a patron saint goes back at least to the Middle Ages and many of the favourite patron saints are represented among house names – along with a few unexpected ones and some who seem to be purely modern inventions.

St Katherine (sometimes appealed to by spinsters in search of a husband) has had houses dedicated to her since at least 1658, and although the custom is perhaps not quite so fashionable today as it was before World War II, there are still many houses bearing saints' names, particularly in areas such as Glastonbury and other centres with strong religious associations. Those 'of sound common sense, sane good humour and generous ideals' have chosen St Theresa's or St Teresa's. St Nicholas is well liked. Apart from his associations with Santa Claus and the custom of giving gifts, he is regarded as the patron saint of children. Most of the St Patrick's are dedicated to the patron saint of Ireland, who also looks after sailors. St Elmo takes particular care of Mediterranean sailors. St Ann, St George, St James – all have cottages, houses and villas under their care, and a number of houses bear the name of St Ninian, who evangelised the Northern Britons and the Picts. St Jude (frequently found in the personal columns of The Times), St Michael (patron saint of policemen), St Adrian (patron saint of soldiers and butchers) and St Edmund (and there were five saints of this name); all these and many more can be seen both in the UK and abroad. One dedication is particularly noteworthy – a coach operator has called his house St Christopher's (the patron saint of travellers).

Occasionally an Ebenezer Cottage can be found attached to what was once an Ebenezer Chapel. The Old Chapel House usually turns out to be a former chapel now renovated and turned into a private home.

Of all the religious references, the most frequently used is Crimond, one of the best known settings to Psalm 23 suggesting that the occupants will be under Divine protection. This can be seen throughout the country. Green Pastures is sometimes used as a reference to this psalm too.

Myths, Legends and Superstition

MYTHS and legends are an appropriate (and sometimes gloriously inappropriate) source of many names. In particular the Arthurian legends provide names for houses all over the world. The most frequently used are Avalon (the Land of the Blessed, the Isle of Souls) which appears not only around Glastonbury where it might be expected, but throughout the world, and Camelot (where Arthur is supposed to have kept the Round Table). Occasionally Pendragon is chosen as a reminder of Arthur's father, Uther Pendragon; Astolat (the dwelling of the maiden rejected by Lancelot, who starved herself to death, also identified with Guildford), Guinevere (Arthur's Queen), Excalibur (Arthur's sword) and even Roundtable Bungalow.

Innisfail is a connection with yet another legend, that of the pillow on which Jacob dreamed.

Janus is particularly appropriate as a house name as,

according to Roman legend, he was the two-faced god of beginnings and doorways, and Janua Caeli, the Door of the Heavens, is equally good, but whether Elysium is a good choice or not rather depends where it has come from. In Greek mythology it refers to the banks of the River Oceanus where the blessed dwell. In Homer the land has no snow, cold or rain and is inhabited by heroes who have been wafted there without dying, but in Roman mythology the Elysian fields were part of the underworld to which the Shades were sent.

Atlantis – the legendary highly civilised isle which disappeared as the result of an earthquake – undoubtedly denotes a mysterious ideal realm, and Nirvana (chosen both here and on the Continent) is a supreme end to effort and longing in Buddhist teaching. Minerva, the goddess of artisans, seems a good choice, but Pandora, who was overcome by temptation and opened the forbidden box, releasing all the evils of life, leaving only Hope behind, is perhaps rarer.

Superstition still plays a part in modern house names – often in quite an imaginative way. Touchwood had a garden adjacent to a small wood and Amulet (a charm which guards against witchcraft and other dangers) was chosen to bring both protection and good luck. However, houses in the course of construction in Britain do not usually have a good luck symbol (such as a branch of fir) attached to the scaffolding as they do on the Continent. Nor, fortunately do our foundations have to be laid in blood, though some who have battled with finance and planning regulations would dispute this. Today we sometimes bury a newspaper and a few common articles under the floor for the enlightenment of future archaeologists and content ourselves with calling the house Talisman, The Mascot or White Heather.

Spooks is close to a churchyard and at least one house is

called The Haunt, but this could be convivial rather than supernatural.

Mizpah can sometimes be seen on a gatepost, although it is more often found engraved inside a ring given as a love token – 'The Lord watch between you and me, when we are absent one from the other'.

In spite of the popularity of horoscopes and the interest in astrology, there are very few house names taken from the signs of the Zodiac.

Witches on broomsticks, black cats and horseshoes, whether we are prepared to admit it or not, are still around, at least on some houses – Witches Moon, Horseshoes, Broomsticks, Mistletoe (which hung over the doorway will prevent the entrance of witches).

Puck, a mischievous household spirit, is responsible for a few names such as Puck's House, Puck's Thatch and Puck's Paigles ('paigles' – cowslips).

Unless Bogeys is used in its golfing or railway sense it is a rather curious choice since a bogey is either an imaginary person or a rather terrifying spirit of hobgoblinish nature. This, however, is outclassed by Bunyip – a bellowing water monster of Australian mythology, said to live at the bottom of lakes and water holes into which it drags its human victims. Gremlin, by comparison, is perhaps somewhat less alarming, as although it was alleged to appear to pilots and aircrews during the two world wars and to cause a lot of trouble, some credited it with bringing airmen back to safety in impossibly damaged planes. I suppose that names akin to Ufo will be next on the list.

The Wish is obviously the fulfilment of a dream and Wishing Well is synonymous with the bringing of good luck, but at Rainbow's End the owners had hoped to find a pot of gold.

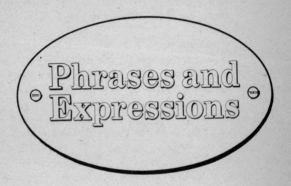

Phrases and Expressions

AN INVOLUNTARY exclamation can sometimes end up in permanent form on the gatepost. Good Heavens resulted from intending owners showing their friends round the barn they proposed to convert into a house. A bit more enthusiasm was engendered at Well Lovely. The Very House catches something of the extreme satisfaction that was felt when the property was first discovered.

Friday While comes from a naval expression for weekend leave (Friday while Sunday) and the use of the word 'while' for 'until' is widespread in parts of the north of England.

Tight Lines makes another good house name, being the expression used by fishermen to wish each other a good catch. Happy Returns is a useful holiday home name. Tally

Ho is sometimes found with an illustrated plaque depicting a hunting scene and Ackybotha resulted from 'Ach! Why bother?'

Of Unknown Origin

IT IS a great pity that more interest has not been taken in the study of house names as already some of them have vanished without trace. Others remain but, as the properties have changed hands, sometimes several times since the houses were named, the origins are now lost. Thus we shall probably never know why Twizzle Twig was so called. Whatever led to Dogdole? Who was the donor of Grace's Gift? Fuzzy Dee is thought to have originated from the first words uttered by the youngest son of the house – but what led him to that? There are new owners at Dragons, but they have no idea why it is so called. Greyne House may well have been a storehouse for grain for the once flourishing local malt trade.

Secondly is certainly not the second house in the road, and it has been concluded that this house must have been the second one to belong to the people who named it.

Although Brandywine is a modern house tucked away on

a Cornish creek, it may well have been built on the site of a smugglers' den, or its first owners may have wished to commemorate the Battle of Brandywine Creek that took place during the American War of Independence, or it could be another name inspired by Tolkien's *The Lord of the Rings* (see page 52), but the origin of this interesting name will probably not now be known as all efforts to trace the people who named it have failed.

Golden Arrow may have had romantic associations with the famous train that used to run from Victoria to Dover – the embarkation point for what were, before the days of the package tour and television, adventures to far away places.

The new owners of Marquis had no idea why their bungalow should have this aristocratic name – unless it was named after the boiler in the kitchen!

The Wardens is something of a puzzle since research into local history has failed to unearth any possible link with guardianship of any kind. The only likely suggestion seems to be that this might have been the home of the local ARP warden during World War II and the name has remained.

It would be incongruous to suggest that The Oval, a beautiful thirteenth century cottage, had any connections with cricket, and it is thought that its name may be a corruption from The Hovel possibly used several centuries ago, although today anything less like a hovel would be hard to imagine.

Disappearing Names

PEOPLE are constantly moving house. Sometimes they take their house name with them if it is of particular personal significance – The Chase (from the stretch of largely unspoilt countryside between Cannock and Stafford) was chosen by a Staffordian for her home in Walton-on-Thames but has now moved with the family to their new house in Felixstowe. Tubberduff moved about the country with its Irish owners. It means The Black Well and was originally the name of the family farm in County Wexford – at the moment it is in a hamlet in Cornwall.

Unfortunately, some splendid names just disappear when their owners move. Boogaloo Junction is no more as its owners have gone abroad and newcomers have chosen another name. The family have moved from Nala-Adnil-Yak (read it backwards). Madurodam (after the miniature village in Holland) has gone. Signals Close used to be owned by a railway enthusiast, but he has moved and the name has disappeared, and the intriguing Bellas Mouse has vanished.

Oop t'nick is a Lancashire expression for a little side entrance, and local history has it that customers entering Ye Olde Vaults, Ashton-under-Lyne, by the alleyway were said to be going 'oop t'nicky'. This highly original name was given, most appropriately, by two people from Lancashire to a house they had built in Cornwall on a narrow piece of land up a lane. Alas, they have now left and the new owners have changed the name to Lanterns.

A few of the very old names have long since vanished for obvious reasons – Hell and Borstal have gone, but Cremlin still remains. Perhaps it is as well that Louse Hall (about 1770) has disappeared completely.

Echoes From the Past

HOUSE names go back through the centuries. Some survive to this day. Some present day names commemorate incidents from history.

Swan Street acquired its name because six hundred years ago it was the first house to be built on the old Roman Swan Street. Fisherman's Hut (which, of course, is nothing of the kind but a large comfortable modern home) has in its garden the remains of a cottage built by a seafaring man on land given to him by the local squire around 1780.

Yeeles House, although fairly new, was built on a field owned by Thomas Yeeles who ran a bakehouse there in the sixteenth century. Honeylands, Worlocks Leaze and Moons Close all take their names from old field names.

Point the Horse is situated at a fork in the main road and in former days when the pack horse team reached this point the leading horse's head was pointed to the right or to the left according to which way the team had to go. This is a superb use of a snippet of history.

In a rather similar manner, Donkey Halt is on a very steep incline at the place where heavily laden donkeys once paused on their way from the beach to the village.

Cockspurs is a sixteenth century cottage, once an inn, which has a very large room where cockfighting is thought to have taken place.

Hatchet and Brandy Cottage is a splendid example of a name with a fascinating story. Legend has it that it was once a storehouse for brandy illicitly brought up from Seaton. When the smugglers realised the Customs and Excise men were on their way they put a hatchet through the barrels. The name was once changed to Valley View, but fortunately the old name has been restored.

According to local legend, The Comedy, a fine mansion near Chippenham, was bought by a gentleman for his mistress, an actress who had scored great success in a play called The Comedy.

$\mathbf{T}$HE world of the wee folk is not confined to children's story books but is alive and well on a great many gateposts. To the forefront are the pixies in many forms – Pixies Nest, Pixies Haunt, Pixies Dell, Pixies Holt, Pixies Halt and Pixies Laughter, and the last name so enchanted the relatives of its owner that they racked their brains for something similar and finally came up with Elfin's Whisper.

In spite of their reputation for being mischievous ugly demons, goblins turn up in house names from time to time, usually in the form of Goblins Glade or Goblins Glen. Dwarf Cottage, Elflands, Little Folk make one reluctant to ring the bell and uncertain who will answer the door. Gnomes Cottage could, in the days of the Gnomes of Zurich, have some financial significance, but otherwise these names leave the caller uncomfortably doubtful whether it is he himself who is pixilated.

There's Many A Slip

CERTAIN names seem to be just right at the moment of naming, but become rather tiresome later on. Snicere (It's nice here) rather lost its point when neighbours insisted on calling it Snikkery. Snogarden, to the uninitiated, looks a little strange until it is realised that there is no garden at all – neither front nor back. Noveston was named in the days when everyone went heavily muffled – there must have been another derivative. Little Onn is definitely after a Midlands village. Although Kirriemuir has literary overtones (it is said to be the origin of J. M. Barrie's *Thrums* – also used as a house name) to the ribald it may have acquired rather different associations.

Changes in fashion can sometimes turn triumph into disaster. In The Lew was named quite appropriately many years ago as 'lew' is a dialect word meaning 'sheltered from the wind' but today the name arouses much the same reaction as could Toulouse and Inverlooe. Little wonder that the houses formerly named Hetts Loo and Bra Cove now bear completely different names. Allmodcons is clearly intentional. Atomia, however, was almost certainly not.

Sometimes a name will be chosen without the owners realising that there is a second, less appropriate meaning. Such is the case at Spartan. The house stands on a narrow rocky ledge well above the village road, and the owners wanted a name that would indicate all the hard work they had endured in hewing out the site. Too late they realised that the word usually brings to mind a frugal or bleak existence.

Amusing or appropriate as they may be, some names can give estate agents nightmares. Imagine trying to sell Swamps Edge, Mire House, Dampach, Crumbledown, Roughit or Rusty Railings. What lies in store for you at Crazydale or Nutters Nest? On the other hand would you really believe Paradise or The Garden of Eden?

It is perhaps unfortunate that today certain names have overtones of the criminal world but this was doubtless far from the minds of those who called their houses Holloway, Newgate and Brixton.

Truckles, Tweakers, Diggins, Grubbins, Little Grunters, Bodgers and Bumblers. It is rather like turning over the leaves of the family photograph album.

How to Run Out of Ideas

IN SPITE of the thousands of existing names to choose from and the infinite variety of sources in the immediate surroundings, some people seem totally devoid of ideas and end up with names which are permanent reminders of lack of inspiration – Idunno, Wedunno, Thistledoo, Thistledous, Thistledome, Noname, Sumware – or, alternatively, Nowhere – satisfy some.

Following an exhaustive, but fruitless search, one owner had had enough and settled for Nuff.

Wit's End and Tether's End are self-explanatory.

Some go to great trouble to convey the idea that they do not really care what they call their houses – Ookares, Wiwurrie, Ynot – perhaps the best of these is Two Hoots.

One way out for some people who just could not find the right name was to settle for The Compromise.

How to Choose a House Name

IF YOU have not found anything in the preceding pages to suit your taste, or you want to have a completely original name (if such a thing is possible – even the very clever ones turn up in more than one place), then there are several ways of approaching the problem.

Consult the oldest map you can find (get the tithe map if it is available) and see whether you can discover the name of the field on which your house was built. Honeylands and Worlocks Leaze resulted from just such a search. Maybe you can find the name of the family who owned the land several centuries ago – Richards Field, Pickles Piece.

Has anything of particular historical interest taken place in your locality – a battle (Sedgemoor, Naseby, Bannockburn), a treaty (Wedmore), an important scientific discovery or an archaeological find? The Local History section at your Public Library should have any books, pamphlets or articles that have been written about your area. The chatty 'scenes from rural life' types of books written a hundred years ago can be very useful. Your County Record Office will be a mine of information.

Are there any notable local personalities you might wish to commemorate? (Hawkstone House was inspired by a local historian, William Hawkstone, who had written a history of the village in which the house was situated.)

Consult one of the excellent reference books on place names and see whether the place where you are now living, or one of the places associated with your family, has a version that might be adapted for your house name – Astede (Ashtead), Eboracum (York), Glevum (Gloucester), Dunelm (Durham), Tepestede (Chipstead).

Look at the location of your house, the ground on which it is built, its main aspect, any particularly striking features in its architecture and what is in its immediate neighbourhood (Barleyclose is quite ingenious).

Many people endeavour to think of a word that sums up some important part of their lives or one which has something to do with the way in which they found their present home. Only you can decide whether you have something in your experience which will enable you to produce a brilliant one-line autobiography. But some of the most striking and memorable names are of this kind.

There may be scope for a play on your own surname, the name of your road or that of the locality. The section on blended names should provide you with food for thought if you are so inclined.

What are your family's interests? Butterfly collection? Fossils? Photography? Fishing? Travelling? A relevant reference book may provide just the right word or phrase for you.

Consider what kind of image you wish to portray on your

notepaper. What will strangers imagine when first reading your house name?

Go and look at the house names around you. What do you think of them? This will give you a starting point and possibly avoid inconvenient duplication.

Then the field is wide open. I hope this book will encourage many new owners to choose a name and by doing so to add something personal, distinctive and perhaps entertaining to the neighbourhood in which they live.

INDEX

A

C

D

E

F

G

H

──────────── I ────────────

M

P

─────────────────── T ───────────────────

--------------------------------- U ---------------------------------

--------------------------------- V ---------------------------------

--------------------------------- W ---------------------------------

---

Y

Z